About the Marine Sanctuaries Conservation Series

The National Oceanic and Atmospheric Administration's Office of National Marine Sanctuaries (ONMS) administers the National Marine Sanctuary Program. Its mission is to identify, designate, protect and manage the ecological, recreational, research, educational, historical, and aesthetic resources and qualities of nationally significant coastal and marine areas. The existing marine sanctuaries differ widely in their natural and historical resources and include nearshore and open ocean areas ranging in size from less than one to over 5,000 square miles. Protected habitats include rocky coasts, kelp forests, coral reefs, sea grass beds, estuarine habitats, hard and soft bottom habitats, segments of whale migration routes, and shipwrecks.

Because of considerable differences in settings, resources, and threats, each marine sanctuary has a tailored management plan. Conservation, education, research, monitoring and enforcement programs vary accordingly. The integration of these programs is fundamental to marine protected area management. The Marine Sanctuaries Conservation Series reflects and supports this integration by providing a forum for publication and discussion of the complex issues currently facing the National Marine Sanctuary Program. Topics of published reports vary substantially and may include descriptions of educational programs, discussions on resource management issues, and results of scientific research and monitoring projects. The series facilitates integration of natural sciences, socioeconomic and cultural sciences, education, and policy development to accomplish the diverse needs of NOAA's resource protection mandate.

Developing Alternatives for Optimal Representation of Seafloor Habitats and Associated Communities in Stellwagen Bank National Marine Sanctuary

Rosamonde R. Cook[1] and Peter J. Auster[2]

[1]U.S. National Park Service, 47050 Generals Highway, Three Rivers, CA, 93271. Email: Rose_Cook@nps.gov

[2]National Undersea Research Center and Department of Marine Sciences, University of Connecticut at Avery Point, 1080 Shennecossett Road, Groton, CT, 06340. Email: Auster@UConn.edu

U.S. Department of Commerce
Carlos M. Gutierrez, Secretary

National Oceanic and Atmospheric Administration
VADM Conrad C. Lautenbacher, Jr. (USN-ret.)
Under Secretary of Commerce for Oceans and Atmosphere

National Ocean Service
John H. Dunnigan, Assistant Administrator

Silver Spring, Maryland
February 2006

Office of National Marine Sanctuaries
Daniel J. Basta, Director

DISCLAIMER

Report content does not necessarily reflect the views and policies of the Office of National Marine Sanctuaries or the National Oceanic and Atmospheric Administration, nor does the mention of trade names or commercial products constitute endorsement or recommendation for use.

REPORT AVAILABILITY

Electronic copies of this report may be downloaded from the National Marine Sanctuaries Program web site at www.sanctuaries.nos.noaa.gov. Hard copies may be available from the following address:

> National Oceanic and Atmospheric Administration
> Office of National Marine Sanctuaries
> SSMC4, N/ORM62
> 1305 East-West Highway
> Silver Spring, MD 20910

COVER

Cover photos: Stellwagen Bank National Marine Sanctuary encompasses a wide diversity of seafloor habitats including mud filled basins (top right), sand and gravel ridges (bottom right), and boulder reefs (left). These habitats support a wide diversity of species representative of the Gulf of Maine region. (Images by P.J. Auster and P. Donaldson, National Undersea Research Center, University of Connecticut).

SUGGESTED CITATION

Cook, R. and P. Auster. 2006. Developing Alternatives for Optimal Representation of Seafloor Habitats and Associated Communities in Stellwagen Bank National Marine Sanctuary. Marine Sanctuaries Conservation Series MSD-05-06. U.S. Department of Commerce, National Oceanic and Atmospheric Administration, Office of National Marine Sanctuaries, Silver Spring, MD. 24 pp.

CONTACT

Peter J. Auster, Ph.D.
Science Director, National Undersea Research Center and
Associate Research Professor, Department of Marine Sciences
University of Connecticut at Avery Point
1080 Shennecossett Rd.
Groton, CT 06340-6048
860-405-9121
peter.auster@uconn.edu

ABSTRACT

The implementation of various types of marine protected areas is one of several management tools available for conserving representative examples of the biological diversity within marine ecosystems in general and National Marine Sanctuaries in particular. However, deciding where and how many sites to establish within a given area is frequently hampered by incomplete knowledge of the distribution of organisms and an understanding of the potential tradeoffs that would allow planners to address frequently competing interests in an objective manner. Fortunately, this is beginning to change. Recent studies on the continental shelf of the northeastern United States suggest that substrate and water mass characteristics are highly correlated with the composition of benthic communities and may therefore, serve as proxies for the distribution of biological biodiversity. A detailed geo-referenced interpretative map of major sediment types within Stellwagen Bank National Marine Sanctuary (SBNMS) has recently been developed, and computer-aided decision support tools have reached new levels of sophistication. We demonstrate the use of simulated annealing, a type of mathematical optimization, to identify suites of potential conservation sites within SBNMS that equally represent 1) all major sediment types and 2) derived habitat types based on both sediment and depth in the smallest amount of space. The Sanctuary was divided into 3610 0.5 min^2 sampling units. Simulations incorporated constraints on the physical dispersion of sampling units to varying degrees such that solutions included between one and four site clusters. Target representation goals were set at 5, 10, 15, 20, and 25 percent of each sediment type, and 10 and 20 percent of each habitat type. Simulations consisted of 100 runs, from which we identified the best solution (i.e., smallest total area) and four near-optimal alternates. We also plotted total instances in which each sampling unit occurred in solution sets of the 100 runs as a means of gauging the variety of spatial configurations available under each scenario. Results suggested that the total combined area needed to represent each of the sediment types in equal proportions was equal to the percent representation level sought. Slightly larger areas were required to represent all habitat types at the same representation levels. Total boundary length increased in direct proportion to the number of sites at all levels of representation for simulations involving sediment and habitat classes, but increased more rapidly with number of sites at higher representation levels. There were a large number of alternate spatial configurations at all representation levels, although generally fewer among one and two versus three- and four-site solutions. These differences were less pronounced among simulations targeting habitat representation, suggesting that a similar degree of flexibility is inherent in the spatial arrangement of potential protected area systems containing one versus several sites for similar levels of habitat representation. We attribute these results to the distribution of sediment and depth zones within the Sanctuary, and to the fact that even levels of representation were sought in each scenario.

KEY WORDS

Marine protected areas, sanctuaries, habitat representation, benthic communities, sediment, fauna, fishing, fisheries, conservation, optimization, MARXAN

TABLE OF CONTENTS

LIST OF FIGURES AND TABLES

INTRODUCTION

The sustainable exploitation of marine fishes and the maintenance of healthy ecosystems can best be achieved in the context of ecosystem management, including measures for the protection of habitats critical for survival, growth, and reproduction of marine organisms (Sherman et al. 1993, Jennings and Kaiser 1998, Peterson et al. 2000). A major form of habitat disturbance to seafloor communities on the continental shelf of New England is the use of bottom-tending mobile gears such as otter trawls and scallop dredges, used to exploit commercially valuable fish and invertebrate populations (Auster et al. 1996, Auster and Langton 1999). Use of these gears, particularly in sensitive habitats, can cause significant and long lasting impacts to the structure of the habitat itself and to the diversity, abundance, and composition of the biological communities living there (Collie et al. 1997). Further, the removal of high trophic level predators, such as Atlantic cod (*Gadus morhua*), can cause trophic cascades that alter the composition and abundance of prey communities associated with the seafloor (Jackson et al. 2001). Hence, both direct and indirect forms of human disturbance can impact biological diversity at both small and large spatial scales.

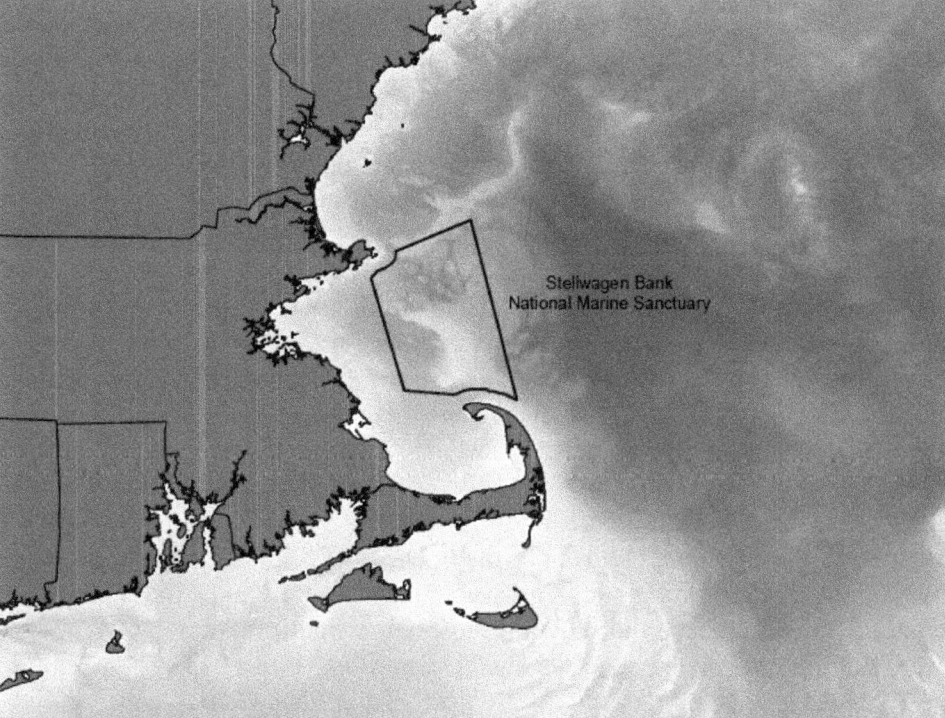

Figure 1. Location of Stellwagen Bank National Marine Sanctuary in the Gulf of Maine. Remote sensing image courtesy of Paskevich, V. 2003. SEAGRD.TIF: Image representation of the NGDC Coastal Relief Model bathymetry for the project area. U.S. Geological Survey, Coastal and Marine Geology Program. Woods Hole Field Center, Woods Hole, Massachusetts.

Stellwagen Bank National Marine Sanctuary (SBNMS), located 25 miles east of Boston in the Gulf of Maine (Figure 1), is the only National Marine Sanctuary within the Acadian biogeographic province of the northeastern United States. While mineral extraction is prohibited under law, current sanctuary regulations do not provide protection for marine communities from most types of fishing, including the use of fishing gears that alter seafloor habitats.

Support has been gaining in recent years among scientists, resource managers, and the public in the United States and other parts of the world for establishing areas in the sea that would receive a level of protection similar to that provided by U.S. National Parks on land, in which all forms of commercial resource extraction is prohibited and anthropogenic disturbance is highly controlled (e.g., Earle et al. 2004). A common theme among calls for greater protection of marine habitats is the identification of areas that would, if protected, preserve a representative portion of a region's biological diversity (e.g., Thackway 1996, National Research Council 2001).

Conservation of marine and terrestrial ecosystems poses different types of challenges (Carr et al. 2003). Protection of terrestrial ecosystems is often constrained by acquisition costs or availability of land, whereas marine conservation, especially in coastal areas, usually requires changes in management regulations that affect various user groups. Large-scale distributions of marine species and communities are also generally lesser known than are those of terrestrial ecosystems. However, recent studies on the continental shelf of the northeastern United States, including portions of SBNMS, suggest that substrate and water mass characteristics are highly correlated with the composition of benthic communities (e.g., Auster et al. 2001, Skinder 2002) and may therefore, serve as proxies for the distribution of biological biodiversity where detailed information on the distributions and abundances of species is lacking. Water mass characteristics have been well defined within the Gulf of Maine and modern tools such as multibeam sonar are improving our ability to map the distribution of seafloor habitats. A detailed geo-referenced interpretative map of major sediment types within SBNMS has recently been developed to aid resource management within the Sanctuary.

Any efforts to increase habitat protection in parts of the SBNMS will likely meet with the greatest success if they attempt to balance the interests of resource users with those of conservation. A good starting point in any such discussion might be to identify the minimum amount of habitat required to preserve representative examples of the Sanctuary's indigenous biological diversity. The purpose of this paper is to demonstrate a means by which this could be done in an objective and transparent manner.

Methods involve the use of a type of mathematical optimization known as simulated annealing, a name that derives from the physical process of heating and slowly cooling a substance to obtain a strong crystalline structure (Kirkpatrick et al. 1983). Simulated annealing is one of several classes of algorithm that have been developed, tested, and applied to real world conservation planning for more than 20 years (see good reviews by Nichols and Margules 1993, Humphries et al. 1996). Most studies have focused on terrestrial applications although similar models have increasingly been used in marine ecoregional planning efforts as well (e.g., Beck and Odaya 2001, Airame et al. 2003, Cook and Auster 2005). Simulated annealing has a variety of advantages over other methods (Pressey et al. 1993), particularly in its ability often to find multiple solutions, or alternate spatial configurations, to meet specific conservation objectives (Possingham et al. 2000). Here we demonstrate the use of simulated annealing as a decision-support tool for identifying potential sets of alternative habitat conservation areas within SBNMS using the map of sediment types described above and a derived set of data for habitats classified by sediment type and depth. Habitat conservation targets were chosen only for demonstration purposes. These and the results presented in this report are not intended as prescriptions for management.

METHODS

The data

Boundaries for SBNMS were digitized from coordinates published in the Federal Register and are stored at the Massachusetts Office of Coastal Zone Management. The marine sediment layer was created by Technology Planning and Management Corporation (TPMC) of Scituate, Massachusetts using multi-beam echo sounder data collected by the United States Geological Survey (Valentine et al. 2001). These data have an accuracy of 10 m^2 and were used to construct a composite seabed backscatter (reflectivity) image of the entire Sanctuary. The strength of the reflectance (gray scale) values is generally associated with the composition of seafloor substrates, with harder substrates producing stronger signals. A digital two-dimensional map of the major sediment types (Figure 2) was generated by defining thresholds for values associated with hard and soft sediments as follows: 1 - 75 for mud, 76 – 165 for sand, and 166 – 255 for gravel.

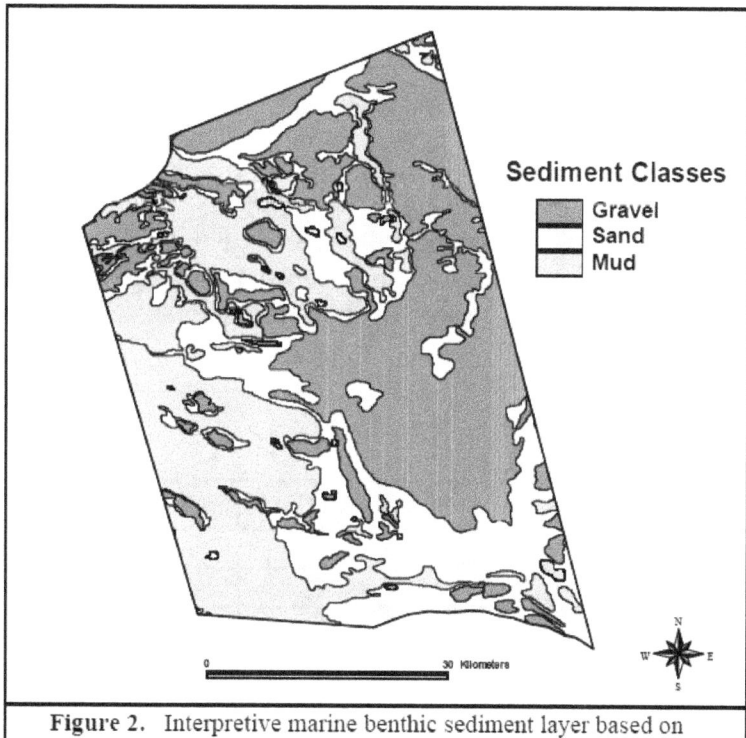

Figure 2. Interpretive marine benthic sediment layer based on reflectance values from multi-beam echo sounder data in Stellwagen Bank National Marine Sanctuary.

We created a map of benthic habitat classes (Figure 3) by reclassifying the sediment layer to include three depth zones (0-60m, 61-150m, and >150m) based on information on the distributions of water masses and fish species assemblages in the Gulf of Maine (Brown et al. 1996, Sherman et al. 1996, Auster 2002).

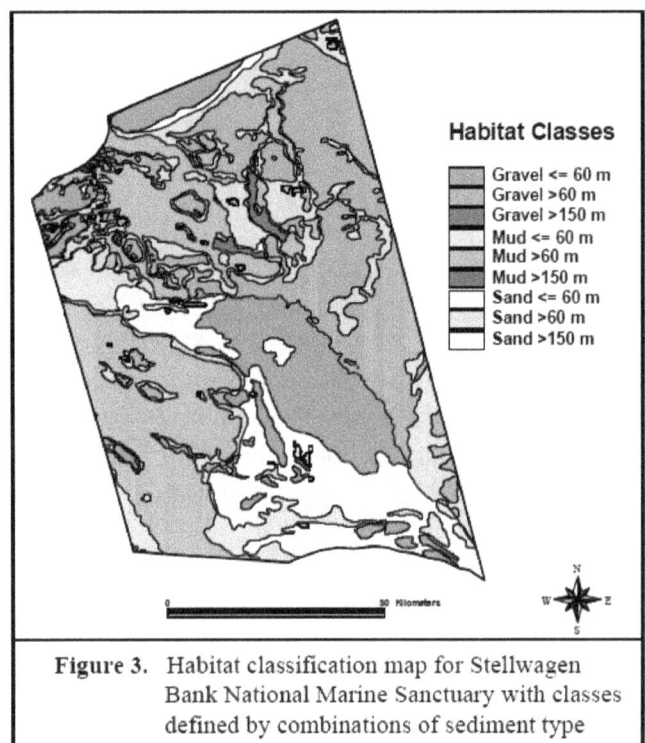

Figure 3. Habitat classification map for Stellwagen Bank National Marine Sanctuary with classes defined by combinations of sediment type (Figure 2) and depth zone.

Overall, gravel represented the most abundant sediment class, with sand and mud present in lesser but approximately equal amounts (Table 1). Most of the Sanctuary (approximately 63%) occurs at depths between 60 and 150m. Gravel and mud were present in approximately equal proportions in this zone, with lesser amounts of sand. Alternatively, sand and gravel were present in roughly equal proportion at depths from 0 to 60m, with lesser amounts of mud. Mud was the most abundant sediment at depths >150m, occupying approximately 77% of substrate area at this depth.

Table 1. Total areal extent of sediment types and habitat classes calculated from the interpretive maps

Depth Range (m)	Gravel (km^2)	Mud (km^2)	Sand (km^2)	Totals (km^2)
All depths	866.1	650.4	674.2	2190.7
Surface to 60	332.2	118.5	330.6	781.3
Between 60 and 150	533.2	516.2	339.5	1388.9
Greater than 150	0.7	15.8	4.2	20.6

4

We sampled the sediment types and habitat classes on the maps by overlaying a grid of 0.5 min squares (described in more detail below) to create a set of sampling units which provided the raw data for the algorithm.

The algorithm

We used MARXAN, Version 1.8 software (Ball and Possingham 2001) to perform simulated annealing, a Monte Carlo procedure used to minimize multivariate functions associated with a physical or biological system. MARXAN's objective function calculates the total cost associated with a set of sampling units as:

$$\text{Total Cost} = \sum_{\text{su's}} \text{SU costs} + \text{BLM} \sum_{\text{su's}} \text{boundary lengths} + \sum_{\text{cf's}} \text{CFPF} * \text{penalty} + \text{Threshold Penalty}$$

where SU refers to sampling units, CFPF to "Conservation Feature Penalty Factor", and BLM to "Boundary Length Modifier". The CFPF weights the cost associated with failure to meet the representation target of each conservation feature specified, these being sediment or habitat types in the present analysis. The threshold penalty represents a cost for exceeding some maximum desired size of solutions.

The BLM is a weighting used to control the spatial aggregation of sampling units, where the boundary length is equal to the sum of the lengths of the sides of sampling units that do not adjoin another unit. If equal to zero, the algorithm performs without spatial constraint. BLM values greater than zero increase the cost of the boundary length and encourage solutions that aggregate sampling units into fewer, compact clusters with shared boundaries. For example, the boundary length of four unconnected squares is 16 (based on all sides of each square), while that of four squares sharing boundaries is 8-10, depending on configuration. The BLM can be adjusted through an iterative process to obtain a desired number of clustered sites.

Simulations are initialized with a set of sampling units drawn at random from the larger data set. Sampling units are then added and removed at random from the set in a long series of iterations, with the total cost of each new set compared to the previous. Changes that reduce the total cost are always retained. Those that do not are accepted with some probability that diminishes over the course of the iterations. The rate of diminishing probability is set by an "annealing schedule" which includes the number of iterations and the number of cooling steps (times the probability of acceptance is reduced). By occasionally accepting changes that increase or do not change the total cost during earlier iterations, the algorithm is able to explore all possible sets, avoiding local optima in search of the global optimum, which will eventually be found given sufficient iterations.

In the present analysis, we wished to identify those parts of the Sanctuary that represent the full diversity of sediment and habitat types in specific quantity (our target levels of representation) in the smallest total area. We set the cost of individual sampling units as equal to their size so that their summed cost was a measure of total included area. We identified the smallest value of the BLM that resulted in solutions that met our target levels of representation in one to four cohesive groups of sampling units (or sites) following the methods described below. We set the threshold penalty to zero and the

CFPF high enough that our targets were always met. In general, larger areas are needed to meet specific representation targets where solutions are constrained to a smaller number of sites. In other words, the fewer sites allowed in solutions, the larger the total included area. Thus, in our analysis, optimization represented a tradeoff between total area and number of sites.

Sampling units

The use of reflectance as a proxy for sediment type is spatial scale-dependent. While there was little correlation between phi values of sediment grab samples and reflectance (P. Valentine personal communication), video observations showed general sediment classification and reflectance values to be highly correlated (e.g., Auster et al. 2001). Based on the latter analysis, we considered it reasonable to assume sampling units of 0.25 min squares or larger would represent sediment types reasonably well.

Therefore, we created three square sampling grids, of 0.25, 0.5, and 1.0 minute latitude and longitude in the geographic coordinate system, and compared these for the effect that sampling scale might have on the outcome of optimization. The grids were clipped to the Sanctuary boundaries such that most sampling units on the boundary consisted of partial squares. The size of whole sampling units varied depending on their position along the north-south and east-west axes being larger at the northern end of the Sanctuary than the southern and in the west than the east, but differences were minor. For example, the greatest difference in size between any two whole 0.5 min squares was 0.006 km^2.

We quantified the amount of each sediment and habitat class per sampling unit by intersecting the data and grid layers, quantifying the areas of the newly created polygons, and summing by class. The sediment and habitat layers were essentially projected against a flat surface to calculate areal coverage. Thus, our estimates of areal coverage do not account for topography and will be underestimated in regions where depth varies. We chose a flat projection because the alternative would have favored the selection of sites with high relief. Such solutions could tend to exclude species with preferences for habitats in low relief environments.

We performed simulations on each data set with target levels of representation equal to 10% and 20% of the three main sediment types. Results obtained with the 0.25 min grid consisted of either many small site clusters (at least nine to ten) or the entire study area. This occurred because the boundaries of planning units on the outer edge of the study area did not count toward the summed cost of the boundary length, and because the combined cost of the sampling units and the boundary length (the total cost score without penalties) rapidly became larger than the cost of all sampling units under even small values of the BLM.

These problems never arose in tests on the 0.5 min and 1.0 min grids. We compared total included area in one, two, and four-site solutions at 10% and 20% target representation levels and chose for comparison the top ten solutions as described in the next section. There was no difference (P > 0.05) between mean total area among any set of solutions at the 10% representation level, or for single-site solutions at 20% representation. Multiple-site solutions obtained with 0.5 min^2 sampling units did however, cover significantly less total area than did those of 1.0 min^2 sampling units (2 sites: F = 13.86, P = 0.002; 4 sites: F = 10.23; P = 0.0056). We therefore chose to use the 0.5 min sampling unit grid, with a total of 3610 sampling units (mean 0.78 km^2), for all subsequent analyses.

Controlling spatial configuration

Boundary lengths were obtained from Arc attribute tables (containing "lpoly" and "rpoly" attributes) following conversion from the shape files containing the sampling unit grids. The boundaries on the outer edge of the Sanctuary were defined as irremovable (Ball and Possingham 2001, page 26). Amounts of each sediment, or habitat, type were transformed to the square root of their original area so that they would scale with the boundary lengths. Thus, total cost, included in the output for each run of the algorithm, is an index of total area. The transformation was necessary in order to keep the values of the BLMs required to obtain a desired number of sites (clustered sampling units) within a reasonable range and had no effect on the outcome.

We performed a large number of experimental simulations to determine the effect that the BLM had on the size of solutions (total included area), their boundary lengths, and number of sampling units. Each trial consisted of 100 runs, as did each of those used to produce the results presented in this report. Each run was performed with 10,000,000 iterations and 50,000 cooling steps. Larger BLM values were associated with a larger range in the number of sampling units among solutions and larger maximum areas, but smaller maximum boundary lengths. Although the boundary length decreased with increasing values of the BLM, the minimum number of sampling units and total included area varied little. The mean number of clusters also varied with the BLM. It was therefore possible to find solutions in which the number of clusters differed but total included area was essentially fixed. That is, for similar total area, solutions could be found that consisted of one or more site clusters. Larger boundary lengths were generally associated with more clusters.

Identifying minimum sets

Identifying a true minimum set of sampling units to meet any representation goal is a difficult mathematical problem. Simulated annealing can find the true minimum given an adequate annealing schedule. For most real-world conservation applications, it is often of little practical value to know the true minimum, as near-minimum sets often come very close and other decision factors will ultimately determine the exact size and location of conservation areas (Kirkpatrick et al. 1983). Furthermore, it is often the case that a greater number of near-minimum versus true minimum sets exists, and this can be an advantage in cases where planners wish to examine a range of alternatives. We present all of the results provided with this report as near-minimum sets. However, the procedure outlined below identified sets that we believe to approximate the true minima.

We defined the "best" solution, out of 100 runs, for any set of inputs to be the one having the fewest sampling units and the smallest boundary length. We used counts of sampling units as a proxy for total area because MARXAN output provides counts of sampling units but not summed area of units and because of the negligible differences in size of whole sampling units. In addition to the best solution, we also identified four "alternates" that were closest to the best in terms of size and boundary length. To identify the smallest number of sampling units needed to represent sediment, or habitat, types at each of the five target levels (5, 10, 15, 20, and 25% of their distribution in the Sanctuary), we ran simulations with BLM values equal to zero. In each case, the set of 100 runs produced solutions with the same number of sampling units. These constituted true minimum sets because the sampling units chosen included only one sediment type each. Site clusters, on the other hand, will include sampling units that span more than one sediment type where the size of clusters exceeds the scale of homogeneity in the substrate map. To approximate true minima in subsequent runs where the BLM was greater than zero, we identified those solutions that contained an equal or near-equal number of sampling units to those obtained with BLM values equal to zero.

It was usually necessary to test a range of BLM values to obtain solutions with one to four site clusters. We started with BLM values equal to one and increased these in regular increments until single-site solutions had a highly rectangular shape (i.e., a minimization of the boundary length). The number of sites identified from each of 100 runs at BLM values identified in this way varied from one and two in some cases to more than two in others. To obtain solutions with more sites, we reduced the BLM in small increments until this was achieved. We were therefore able to identify multiple-site solutions with the smallest boundary lengths (i.e., those with highly rectangular shapes). We sorted results of all runs by their boundary lengths. Boundary lengths were highly correlated with the number of site clusters, so it was a simple matter to identify the smallest boundary length that corresponded with the desired number of sites. We chose as best and alternates, solutions with the smallest boundary lengths and number of sampling units closest to the minimum identified from runs with BLM = 0.

For simulations with habitat classes, we followed a slightly different procedure because total included area and the number of site clusters were not as tightly associated as they had been for the three sediment classes. In these cases, we ordered the results by boundary length and chose as best and alternative solutions, those that had the fewest sampling units for a given number of site clusters.

RESULTS

Here we present results for simulations run with target representation levels of 5, 10, 15, 20, and 25% of each sediment type and 10 and 20% of each habitat class. These were adequate to demonstrate the general patterns that emerged with the application of simulated annealing to our two data sets.

Representation targets were met in all simulations. Multiple solutions existed in every case, with sampling units aggregated into one or more site clusters. Of these, we plotted the best solutions obtained for each representation level and number of sites for sediment types (Figure 4) and habitat classes (Figure 5).

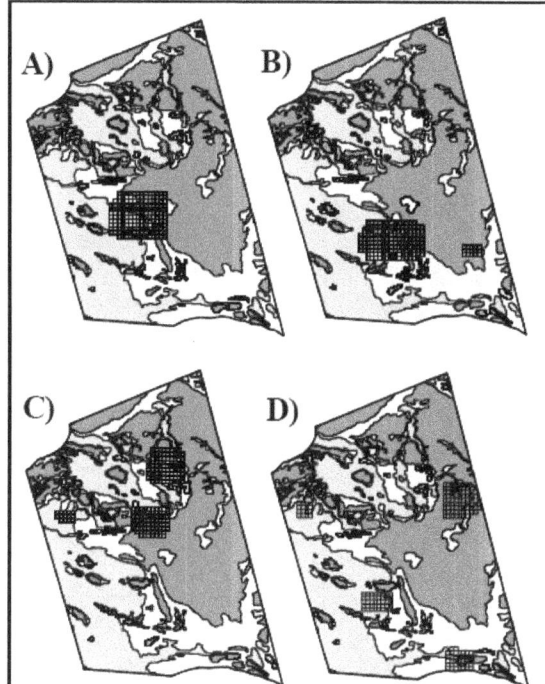

Figure 4.1. Best results, as defined in this report, for 5% representation of each sediment type, distributed among A: 1 site cluster, B: 2 site clusters, C: 3 site clusters, and D: 4 site clusters.

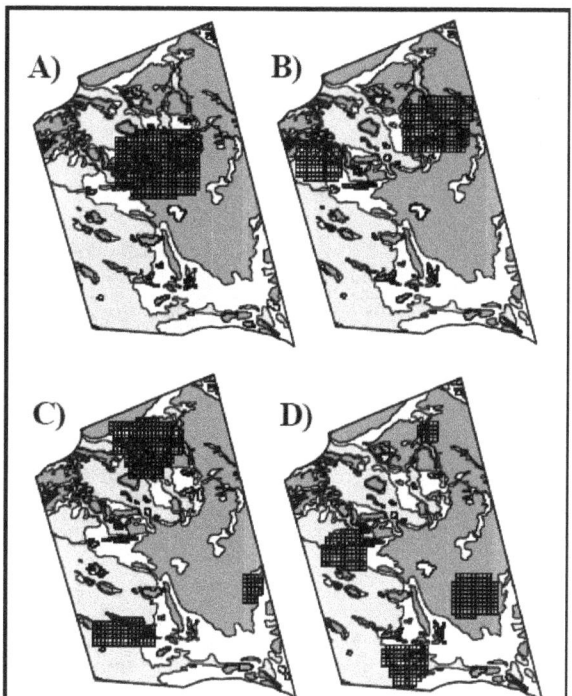

Figure 4.2. Best results, as defined in this report, for 10% representation of each sediment type, distributed among A: 1 site cluster, B: 2 site clusters, C: 3 site clusters, and D: 4 site clusters.

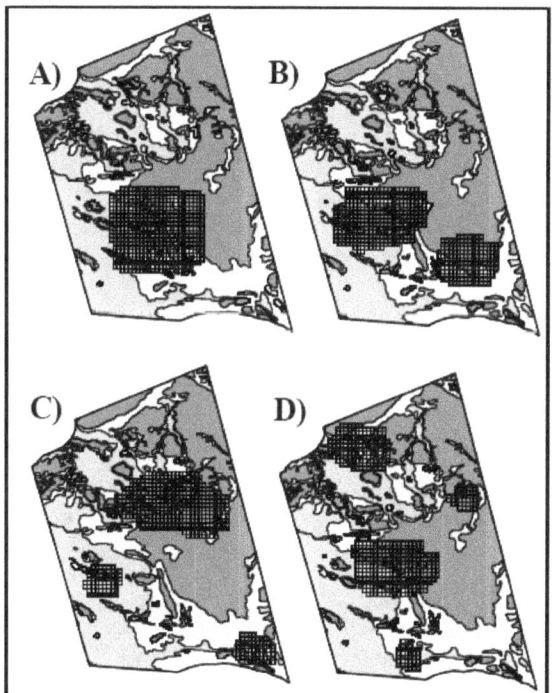

Figure 4.3. Best results, as defined in this report, for 15% representation of each sediment type, distributed among A: 1 site cluster, B: 2 site clusters, C: 3 site clusters, and D: 4 site clusters.

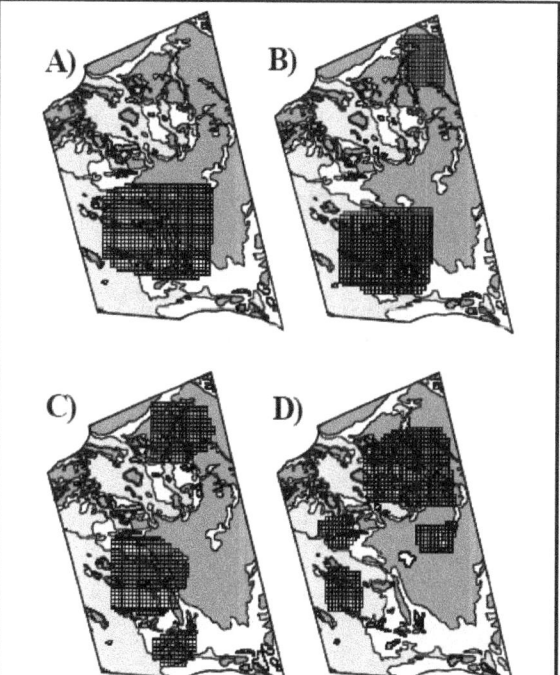

Figure 4.4. Best results, as defined in this report, for 20% representation of each sediment type, distributed among A: 1 site cluster, B: 2 site clusters, C: 3 site clusters, and D: 4 site clusters.

9

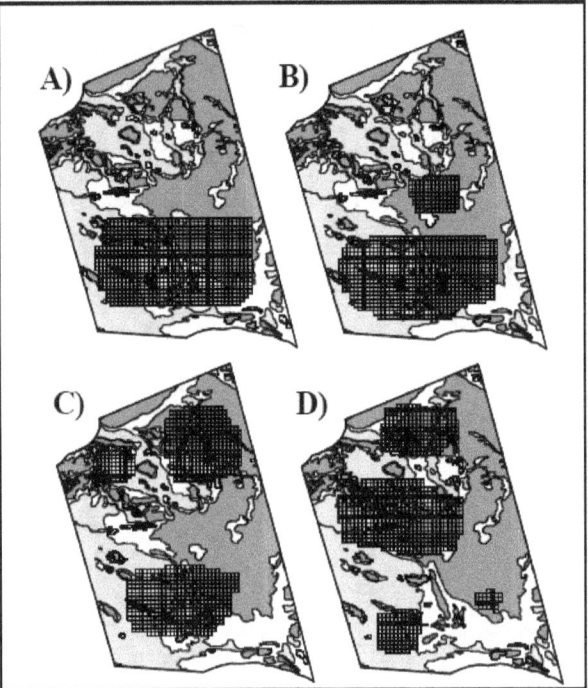

Figure 4.5. Best results, as defined in this report, for 25% representation of each sediment type, distributed among A: 1 site cluster, B: 2 site clusters, C: 3 site clusters, and D: 4 site clusters.

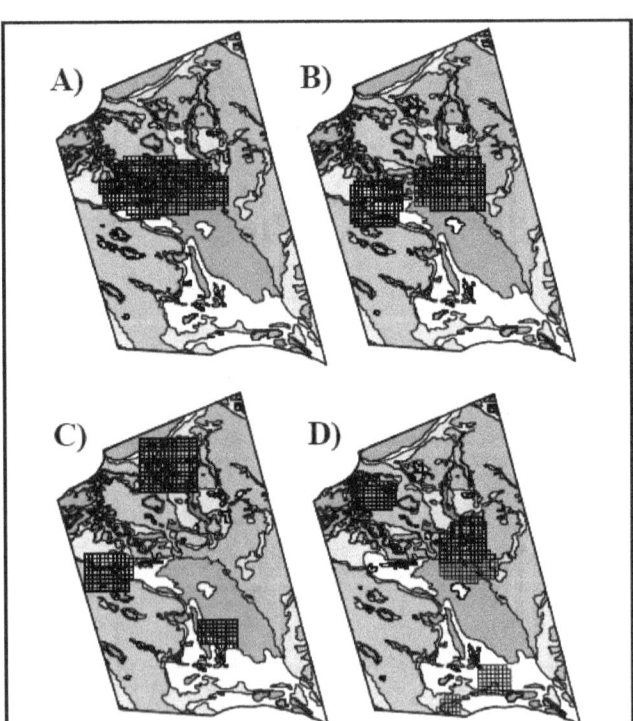

Figure 5.1. Best results, as defined in this report, for 10% representation of each habitat type, distributed among A: 1 site cluster, B: 2 site clusters, C: 3 site clusters, and D: 4 site clusters.

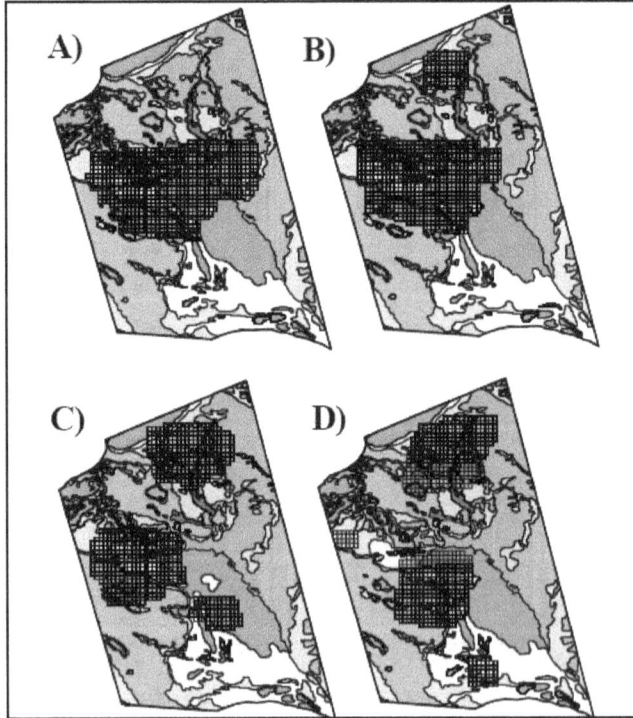

Figure 5.2. Best results, as defined in this report, for 20% representation of each habitat type, distributed among A: 1 site cluster, B: 2 site clusters, C: 3 site clusters, and D: 4 site clusters.

Mean percent area of the entire Sanctuary in solutions from each set of 100 runs on the sediment data was equal to the percent representation of each sediment type, with a mean standard deviation from all runs of 0.011 (range: 0.003-0.048). Thus, for example, with minor deviation, the outcome of runs for which 10% of each sediment type was represented covered 10% of the area of the Sanctuary. This relationship did not vary with the number of site clusters. Results were similar where the nine habitat classes were represented except that total included area was slightly greater on average (but less than 1% of the area of the Sanctuary) than representation levels for solutions with one or two sites. Mean standard deviation from these runs was 0.112 with a range of 0.004-.378, somewhat higher than those obtained with the sediment data.

Boundary length increased in direct proportion to number of sites at all levels of representation for simulations with the sediment (Figure 6) and habitat data (Figure 7). However, boundary lengths increased more rapidly with number of sites at higher levels of representation (Figure 8).

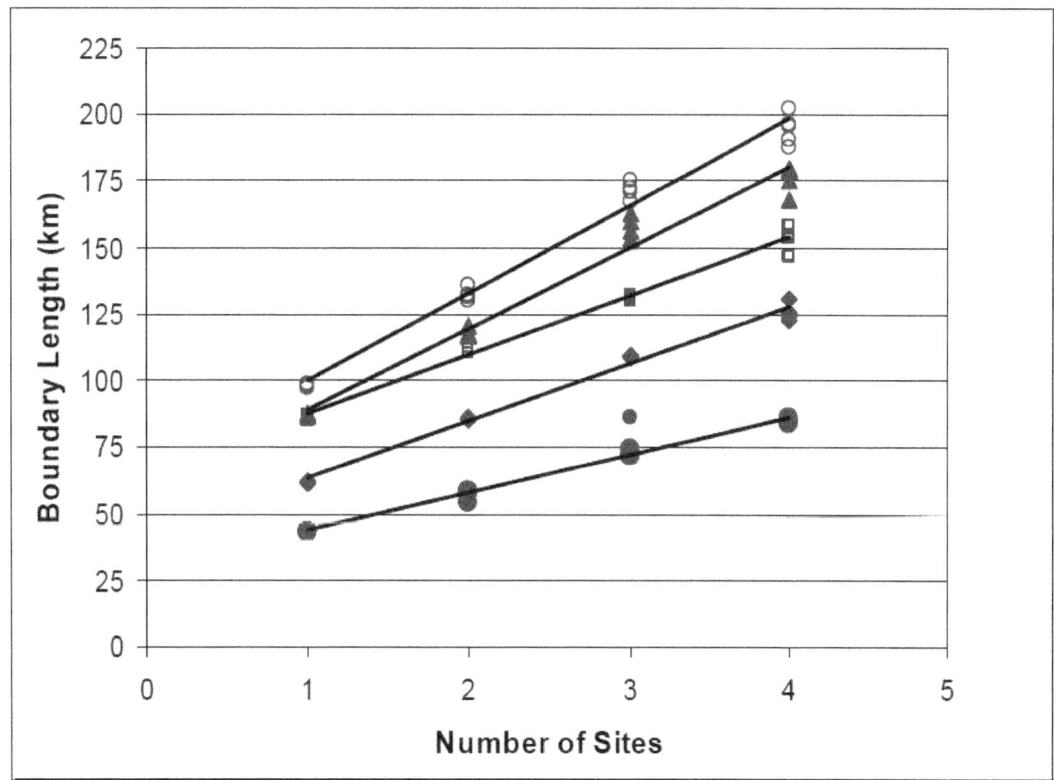

Figure 6. Boundary length as a function of the number of sites for best and alternate solutions of 5% (⊙), 10% (◇), 15% (□), 20% (▲), and 25% (○) representation of sediment types.

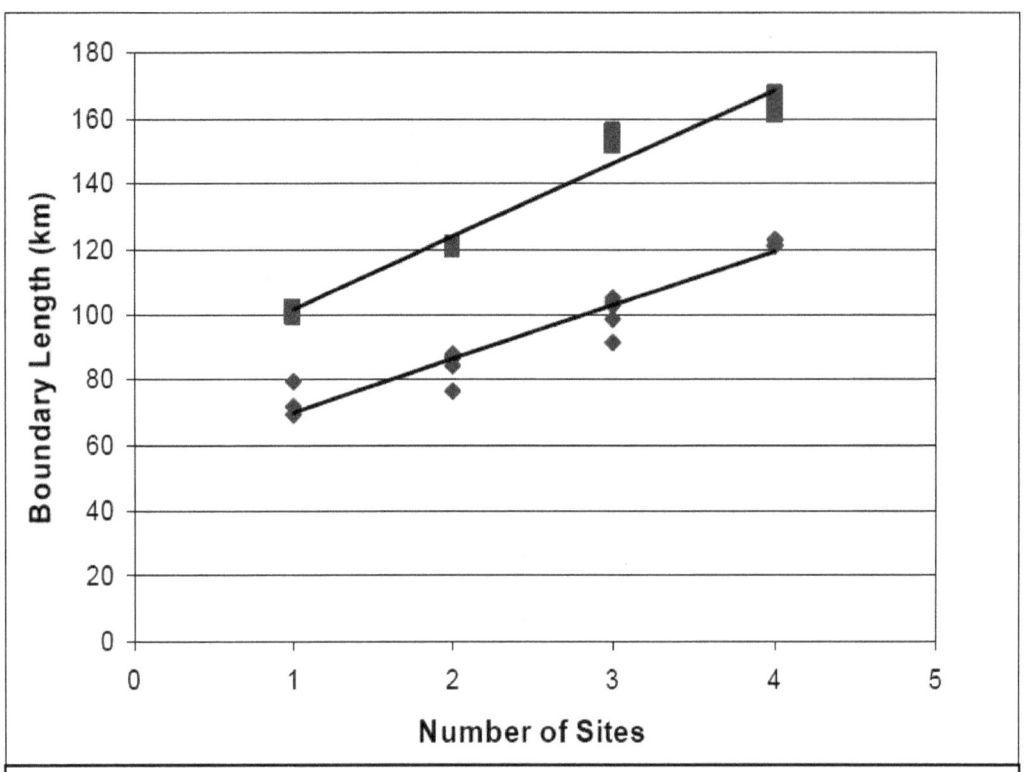

Figure 7. Boundary length as a function of the number of sites for best and alternate solutions of 10% (◇) and 20% (▨) representation of habitat classes.

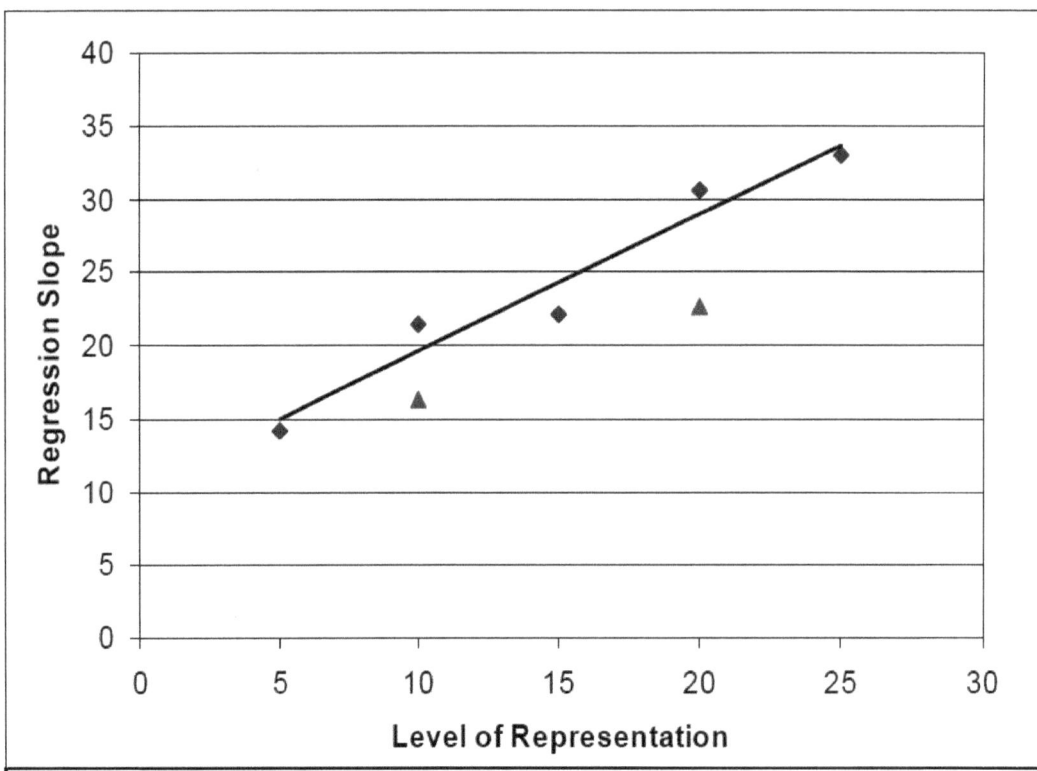

Figure 8. Slope of regression equations versus number of sites for the relationships shown in Figure 6 (◇) and Figure 7 (△).

Differences in total area between the best and alternate solutions for sediment types were no more than 1 km^2, although differences in boundary length were as much as 15 km or 8% longer (Table 2). By contrast, differences in total area between the best and alternate solutions for habitat classes were as much as 21 km^2, but still only about 1% of the total area of the Sanctuary. Differences in boundary length were at most 12 km (Table 3).

Table 2. Boundary Length Modifier (BLM), run number, total area (in km^2), and boundary length (BL) (in km) of the best and four alternate solutions as defined in this report for 5, 10, 15, 20, and 25% representation of three sediment classes under four spatial configurations.

	5%				10%				15%				20%				25%			
	BLM	Run	Area	BL	BLM	Run	Area	BL	BLM	Run	Area	BL	BLM	Run	Area	BL	BLM	Run	Area	BL
1 site																				
Best	25	15	110	43	5	35	219	62	10	59	329	107	10	45	439	87	10	22	548	97
Alt1	25	98	110	43	5	42	219	62	10	55	329	154	10	72	439	87	10	2	548	97
Alt2	25	46	110	43	5	89	219	62	10	26	329	154	10	73	438	87	10	35	548	98
Alt3	25	64	110	43	5	6	218	62	10	87	329	170	10	54	439	87	10	28	548	98
Alt4	25	50	110	43	5	53	219	62	10	95	329	107	10	14	439	87	10	68	548	98
2 sites																				
Best	25	22	110	54	5	72	219	85	10	16	329	110	10	1	438	117	10	96	548	130
Alt1	25	12	109	57	5	38	219	86	10	20	329	112	10	6	438	117	10	21	548	131
Alt2	25	75	110	58	5	17	219	86	10	51	329	113	10	46	438	117	10	58	548	133
Alt3	25	38	110	58	5	19	219	86	10	29	329	113	10	61	438	120	10	10	548	136
Alt4	25	37	110	58	5	100	220	86	10	20	329	112	10	48	438	121	10	49	548	136
3 sites																				
Best	10	76	110	71	0.5	10	219	109	1	96	329	130	0.5	99	438	153	1	28	548	167
Alt1	10	93	109	71	0.5	65	218	109	1	27	329	130	0.5	69	438	154	1	47	548	171
Alt2	10	99	109	71	0.5	87	218	109	1	98	329	131	0.5	13	438	157	1	97	548	171
Alt3	10	79	109	86	0.5	84	218	109	1	3	329	131	0.5	30	438	160	1	18	548	172
Alt4	10	37	110	74	0.5	58	219	110	1	1	329	132	0.5	2	438	163	1	29	548	175
4 sites																				
Best	1	83	110	84	0.5	32	219	123	1	19	329	147	0.5	83	438	168	1	36	548	188
Alt1	1	43	110	84	0.5	88	219	124	1	55	329	154	0.5	31	438	176	1	22	548	191
Alt2	1	98	110	85	0.5	1	219	125	1	26	329	154	0.5	81	438	179	1	62	548	197
Alt3	1	38	110	85	0.5	16	219	125	1	33	329	155	0.5	88	438	179	1	50	548	203
Alt4	1	35	110	86	0.5	41	219	131	1	94	326	158	0.5	66	438	180	1	15	548	196

Table 3. Boundary Length Modifier (BLM), run number, total area, and boundary length (BL) of the best and four alternate solutions as defined in this report for 10 and 20% representation of nine habitat types under four spatial configurations.

	10%				20%			

1 site

	BLM	Run	Area	BL	BLM	Run	Area	BL
Best	20	96	233	72	30	29	454	102
Alt1	20	90	233	72	30	20	454	101
Alt2	20	73	234	80	30	10	457	101
Alt3	20	83	235	70	30	27	457	102
Alt4	20	54	235	70	30	2	464	99

2 sites

	BLM	Run	Area	BL	BLM	Run	Area	BL
Best	10	45	221	87	30	55	448	120
Alt1	10	10	225	87	30	8	449	121
Alt2	10	21	225	88	30	50	452	122
Alt3	10	88	227	76	30	81	456	120
Alt4	10	24	227	85	30	33	469	121

3 sites

	BLM	Run	Area	BL	BLM	Run	Area	BL
Best	10	81	220	104	1	13	439	152
Alt1	10	5	221	105	1	26	439	152
Alt2	10	33	221	103	1	72	439	156
Alt3	10	64	225	98	1	9	439	154
Alt4	10	44	228	92	1	45	439	152

4 sites

	BLM	Run	Area	BL	BLM	Run	Area	BL
Best	1	28	219	121	1	41	439	161
Alt1	1	27	220	123	1	12	439	166
Alt2	1	7	220	123	1	57	439	168
Alt3	1	3	220	121	1	82	439	167
Alt4	1	61	221	121	1	18	439	162

It is evident that the locations of sites selected by the algorithm varied among solutions, depending on representation level, number of clusters, and area included. However, the probability of selection varied among individual sampling units and cluster sites, and therefore some sampling units and sites were represented more frequently in solutions that others. We can represent frequency of inclusion by plotting summed solutions in which the number of times each sampling unit is included in a solution is summed over all runs and displayed as a graded color scheme. MARXAN will output summed solutions if specified.

We plotted summed solutions from four simulations to illustrate the range of variation in spatial configuration of alternate solutions and how this varies with the target number of sites (Figure 9).

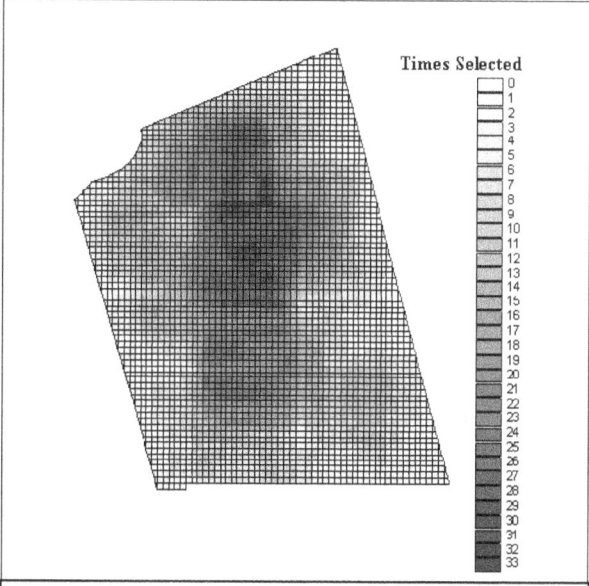

Figure 9.1. The summed solution for 100 runs of a MARXAN simulation. Target representation levels were 10% of each sediment type. The BLM was 5. Times selected is the number of times that a sampling unit was included in a solution set.

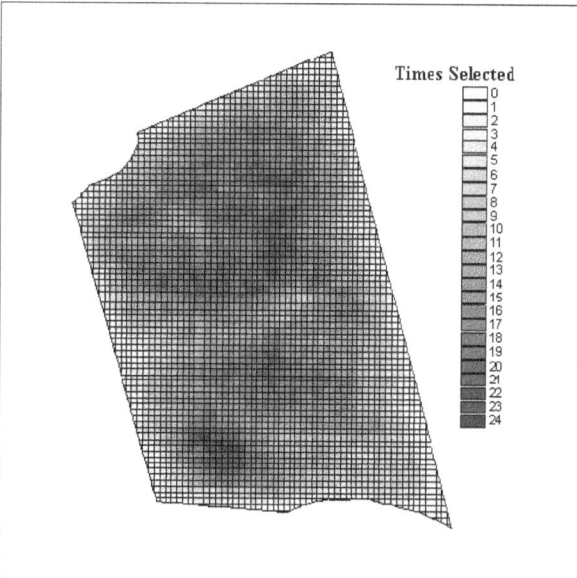

Figure 9.2. The summed solution for 100 runs of a MARXAN simulation. Target representation levels were 10% of each sediment type. The BLM was 0.5. Times selected is the number of times that a sampling unit was included in a solution set.

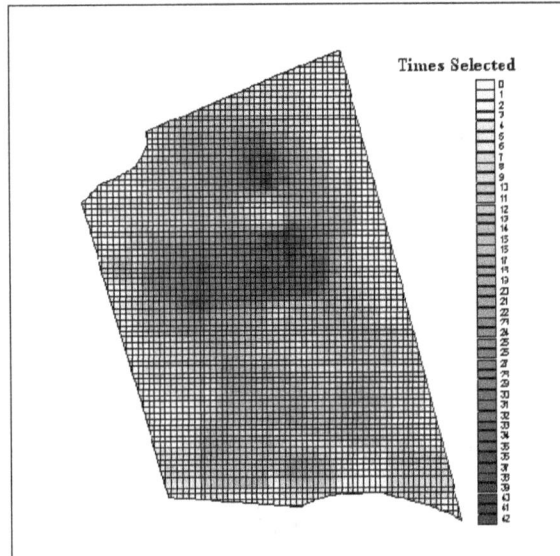

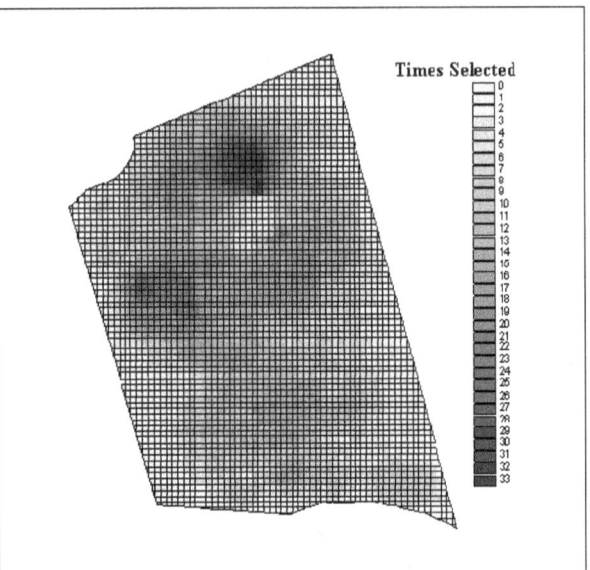

| **Figure 9.3.** | The summed solution for 100 runs of a MARXAN simulation. Target representation levels were 10% of each habitat class. The BLM was 10. Times selected is the number of times that a sampling unit was included in a solution set. | **Figure 9.4.** | The summed solution for 100 runs of a MARXAN simulation. Target representation levels were 10% of each sediment type. The BLM was 1. Times selected is the number of times that a sampling unit was included in a solution set. |

Simulations producing mostly one and two-site solutions exhibited less variation in the location of sites selected across runs and fewer sampling units with a moderate to high probability of being selected. Differences were most pronounced among simulations where sediment rather than habitat type representation was the goal. The outcome of simulations on the sediment data further exhibited a tighter clustering of moderate to high probability sampling units in the center region of the Sanctuary (Figure 9.1) compared to simulations producing three- and four-site solutions (Figure 9.2). Differences were less pronounced among simulations targeting representation of the nine habitat types (Figure 9.3 and Figure 9.4).

DISCUSSION

Results of this analysis suggest a great deal of flexibility in the selection of protected areas for equal representation of benthic habitats in SBNMS. Not only do targeted levels of representation of sediment types and habitat classes, expressed in terms of percent cover, correlate strongly with percent of the study area needed to represent them in a minimal amount of space, but this area remains fairly constant under a variety of spatial design scenarios. These patterns are consistent over a range of representation levels as well.

These patterns were not anticipated and differ from results reported in a similar analysis but using abundance distribution data of demersal fishes from research trawl surveys across the eastern continental shelf of the United States (Cook and Auster 2005). The most likely explanation for the present results is that each of the three sediment types occurred in roughly equal proportions within the Sanctuary and there was a good mix of all three in most areas. Thus, solutions were very efficient in that none of the targeted amounts of sediment or habitat types were exceeded in order to adequately represent all of them under the spatial constraints imposed (one to four sites). There was likely less spatial variation among simulations targeting habitat versus sediment type representation because deep-water habitats (>150m) are much more localized within the Sanctuary than are the others. Nevertheless, the additional cost of representing the nine habitat classes versus three sediment types in terms of total included area was quite small (less than 1% more of Sanctuary area).

Although the total habitat area included in solutions was not affected by aggregation, boundary length increased in direct proportion to the number of sites, given a constant representation of sediment and habitat types. Thus, all things being equal, total boundary length and boundary to area ratio would be smaller for conservation strategies that emphasized a single protected area versus those that allocated the same amount of habitat area among two or more sites. A single large protected area might be favored over several smaller ones for a number of reasons (see Fogarty 1999 and Dayton et al. 2000 for good discussions). Among these, smaller boundary lengths can reduce social and economic impacts of habitat protection as well as the difficulty and expense of enforcement. Smaller boundary-to-area ratios also tend to reduce movement rates of mobile organisms from inside to out (Polacheck 1990, Lindholm et al. 2001), thus larger areas may offer more protection to their inhabitants, particularly if exploitation occurs right on the boundaries. On the other hand, multiple sites increase both redundancy and the likelihood of including greater biodiversity. Since boundary length increases faster with number of sites at higher levels of representation, a preferred design strategy might differ depending on how much habitat were to be protected.

Each of the 100 runs of a simulation represents an optimal or near-optimal solution to a set of representation targets given the constraints defined by the optimization function. Near-optimal solutions varied little from the best (optimal) solutions in terms of total area and boundary length. Therefore, each of the 100 runs of a simulation could be viewed as a good solution, where 'good' is defined in terms of a conservative use of space in representing sediment type diversity. The summed solutions provide an indication of how much flexibility exists in the number and location of these solutions.

In SBNMS, there are fewer good one- and two-site solutions than three- and four-site solutions to the equal representation of sediment types because of the distribution of sediments. Sediment type heterogeneity is highest toward the center of the Sanctuary. Therefore, simulations constrained by the BLM to produce one- and two- site solutions will be concentrated in this area because this is where equal representation can be achieved most efficiently (note however, that if representation goals had not been equal, these results might have been quite different). Since the three sediment types are broadly distributed within the Sanctuary, efficient representation can be achieved through a large number of different spatial configurations. Thus, greater flexibility in spatial configuration is achieved with a greater number of sites.

However, the choice of sites based on sediment type alone would ignore the relationships that many organisms have with habitats defined by a greater number of physical and biological factors. Depth is an important, although not necessarily the only other, determinate of distribution for many marine organisms. Results of the our analysis indicate that considerably less variability exists in the number of potential sites, where representation must include each of the nine habitat classes defined by our three sediment types and depth zones. These are concentrated in the central portion of the northern half of the Sanctuary because this is the only area where three habitat types occur at depths exceed 150 meters. Even when the BLM allows for more than 2 sites, most solutions will include one or more in this region, although there will likely exist greater flexibility in the location of the other sites.

The underlying assumption in this study is that patterns in the distribution of species and communities are highly correlated with sediment type and water temperature and these factors can serve as proxies for representative communities of organisms. Such patterns have been demonstrated for both fishes (Langton et al. 1995, Brown et al. 1996, Auster et al. 1998, 2001, 2002) and benthic invertebrates (Kostylov et al. 2001, Skinder 2002) in the Gulf of Maine and are common patterns for a wide range of benthic and demersal taxa in other parts of the world ocean (e.g., MaCall and Tevesz 1982, Etter and Grassle 1992, Morrisey et al. 1992, Zajac et al. 2000). For example, sea pens (*Pennaltula acculeata*) are common structure-forming fauna in deep mud habitats (mud sediment type and Maine deep water) of SBNMS (Auster unpublished data). Use of only sediment type as a habitat attribute reduces the probability of inclusion of this species in any management scheme focused on representation. Use of sediment type and temperature as a proxy for habitat in conservation planning, in the absence of robust data on the distribution and abundance of fauna at the spatial scales of individual protected areas, allows managers to develop conservation alternatives in a precautionary manner (sensu Auster et al. 1997) to meet goals for the conservation and sustainable use of biological diversity within National Marine Sanctuaries.

The purpose of this study was to demonstrate the utility of simulated annealing as a decision support tool for resource management planning in SBNMS and to examine some of the general patterns discovered in an application that varied representation of marine habitats within the range often advocated for regional inclusion in marine protected areas (National Research Council 2001). There are several ways in which the present analysis could be expanded or improved.

First, we made the simplifying assumption that the "cost" of sampling units was directly proportional to their size. In so doing, we were able to directly compare tradeoffs in total area and spatial structure of solutions equivalent in habitat representation. In future analyses, the cost function could be expanded to include additional social or economic terms, such as those related to commercial and recreational fishing, with appropriate values assigned to individual sampling units. Weighting factors could be applied to these terms in order to evaluate the effects on solutions and the trade-offs associated with one or more of these factors.

Secondly, boulder pile and rocky reef habitats were not included in our sediment data. These relatively localized habitats cannot be distinguished easily from other gravel substrates using multi-beam data. However, it is possible to interpret pattern in gray scale to differentiate boulder and reef habitats based on small-scale patterns in variation of reflectivity. A map product has been developed based on visual interpretation of the multibeam record (P. Valentine unpublished data) but was not completed in time for use in the present study. Auster et al. (1998) showed that the composition and abundance of fishes differed between gravel and boulder reef-dominated habitats, so subsequent analyses should differentiate between these habitats to provide a more complete range of sediment types, and by extension, of biological diversity.

Finally, use of habitat or species-specific research results, as well as traditional ecological knowledge (e.g., from the fishing community), could be used to prioritize habitats in this type of analysis. For example, known habitat patches (planning units) that are important for key species (e.g., locations of nursery or spawning habitat) can be identified a priori to be included in any solution. Such planning units can be selected for species of ecological or economic importance as well as those that are sensitive to disturbance, rare or are of particular interest to managers or the public.

There are several ways to develop alternatives for spatial management regimes in marine protected areas. These include methods where stakeholders develop a priori maps with defined management units and defend their assumptions or priorities represented by each. Final solutions require iterative renditions based on changing sets of assumptions and priorities. Simulated annealing using MARXAN or related programs provides managers and stakeholders with a tool that can incorporate a priori ecological, economic, and other societal priorities in a manner that precedes the display of solutions. Such an approach can garner results that are acceptable to diverse user groups as the variety of optimal solutions represents the amalgam of stakeholder requirements.

ACKNOWLEDGEMENTS

We thank Craig MacDonald and Benjamin Cowie-Haskell for permission to use the sediment data layer, Hugh Possingham and Ian Ball for permission to use MARXAN, Technology Planning and Management Corporation for technical assistance, Kevin Joy for generating the boundary length data, Rikki Grober-Dunsmore and an anonymous referee for helpful suggestions, and Kathy Dalton for editing the manuscript. RC was supported by a grant from Environmental Defense. PA was supported by NOAA's Undersea Research Program, Stellwagen Bank National Marine Sanctuary and the Census of Marine Life Gulf of Maine Program. The views expressed herein are those of the authors and do not necessarily reflect the views of the funding agencies.

LITERATURE CITED

Airame, S., J.E. Dugan, K.E. Lafferty, H.M. Leslie, D.A. McArdle, and R.R. Warner. 2003. Applying ecological criteria to marine reserve design: a case study from the California Channel Islands. Ecological Applications. 13S:S170-S184.

Auster, P.J. 2002. Representation of biological diversity of the Gulf of Maine region at Stellwagen Bank National Marine Sanctuary (Northwest Atlantic): patterns of fish diversity and assemblage composition. Pages 1096-1125 in S. Bondrup-Nielson, T. Herman, N.W.P. Munro, G. Nelson and J.H.M. Willison, editors. Managing Protected Areas in a Changing World. Science and Management of Protected Areas Association, Wolfville, Nova Scotia.

Auster, P.J., K. Joy, and P.C. Valentine. 2001. Fish species and community distributions as proxies for seafloor habitat distributions: the Stellwagen Bank National Marine Sanctuary example (Northwest Atlantic, Gulf of Maine). Environmental Biology of Fishes 60:331-346.

Auster, P.J., and R.W. Langton. 1999. The effects of fishing on fish habitat. American Fisheries Society Symposium 22:150-187.

Auster, P.J., C. Michalopoulos, P.C. Valentine, and R.J. Malatesta. 1998. Delineating and monitoring habitat management units in a temperate deep-water marine protected area. Pages 169-185 in N.W.P. Munro and J.H.M. Willison, editors. Linking Protected Areas with Working Landscapes, Conserving Biodiversity. Science and Management of Protected Areas Association, Wolfville, Nova Scotia.

Auster, P.J., L. Watling, and A. Rieser. 1997. Comment: The interface between fisheries research and habitat management. North American Journal of Fisheries Management 17:591-595.

Auster, P.J., R.J. Malatesta, R.W. Langton, L. Watling, P.C. Valentine, C. Lee, S. Donaldson, E. Langton, A.N. Shepard, and I.G. Babb. 1996. The impacts of mobile fishing gear on seafloor habitats in the Gulf of Maine (northwest Atlantic): Implications for conservation of fish populations. Reviews in Fisheries Science 4:185-202.

Ball, I.R. and H.P. Possingham. 2001. MARXAN – A Reserve System Selection Tool. Available from H. P. Possingham, The Ecology Center, University of Queensland, Brisbane, Australia, or worldwide web site: www.ecology.uq.au/marxan.htm.

Beck, M.W. and M. Odaya. 2001. Ecoregional planning in marine environments: identifying priority sites for conservation in the northern Gulf of Mexico. Aquatic Conservation 11:235-242.

Brown, S.K., R. Mahon, K.C.T. Zwanenburg, K.R. Buja, L.W. Claflin, R.N. O'Boyle,

B. Atkinson, M. Sinclair, G. Howell, and M.E. Monaco. 1996. East Coast of North America groundfish: Initial explorations of biogeography and species assemblages. Silver Spring, MD: National Oceanic and Atmospheric Administration, and Dartmouth, NS: Department of Fisheries and Oceans.

Carr, M.H., J.E. Neigel, J.A. Estes, S. Andelman, R.R. Warner, and J.L. Largier. 2003. "Comparing marine and terrestrial ecosystems: Implications for the design of coastal marine reserves." Ecological Applications 13(1):S90-S107.

Collie, J.S., G.A. Escanero, and P.C. Valentine. 1997. Effects of bottom fishing on benthic megafauna of Georges Bank. Marine Ecology Progress Series 155:159-172.

Cook, R.R. and P.J. Auster. 2005. Use of simulated annealing for identifying essential fish habitat in a multispecies context. Conservation Biology 19:876-886.

Dayton, P.K., E. Sala, M.J. Tegner, and S. Thrush. 2000. Marine reserves: parks, baselines, and fishery enhancement. Bulletin of Marine Science 66:617–634.

Earle, S.A., R. Chandler, L. Madin, S.M. Malcom, G.P. Nabhan, P. Raven, and E.O. Wilson. 2004. National Park Service Science in the 21st Century: Recommendations Concerning Future Directions for Science and Scientific Resource Management in the National Parks. A National Parks Science Committee Report to the National Park System Advisory Board. National Park Service Office of Policy, U.S. Department of the Interior.

Etter, R.J. and J.F. Grassle. 1992. Patterns of species diversity in the deep sea as a function of sediment particle size diversity. Nature 360:576-578.

Fogarty, M.J. 1999. Essential habitat, marine reserves, and fishery management. Trends in Ecology and Evolution 14:133-134.

Humphries, C.J., C.R. Margules, R.L. Pressey, and R.I Vane-Wright. 1996. Priority areas analysis: systematic methods for conserving biodiversity. Oxford University Press, Oxford.

Jackson, J.B.C., M.X. Kirby, W.H. Berger, K.A. Bjorndal, L.W. Botsford, B.J. Bourque, R.H. Bradbury, R. Cooke, J. Erlandson, J.A. Estes, T.P. Hughes, S. Kidwell, C.B. Lange, H.S. Lenihan, J.M. Pandolfi, C.H. Peterson, R.S. Steneck, M.J. Tegner, and R.R. Warner. 2001. Historical overfishing and the recent collapse of coastal ecosystems. Science 293: 629–38.

Jennings, S. and M.J. Kaiser. 1998. The effects of fishing on marine ecosystems. Advances in Marine Biology 34:201-351.

Kirkpatrick, S., C.D. Gelatt Jr., and M.P. Vecchi. 1983. Optimization by simulated annealing. Science 220:671-680.

Kostylov, V.E., B.J. Odd, G.B.J. Fader, R.C. Courtney, G.D.M. Cameron, and R.A. Pickrill. 2001. Benthic habitat mapping on the Scotian Shelf based on multibeam bathymetry, surficial geology and sea floor photographs. Marine Ecology Progress Series 219:121-137.

Langton, R.W., P.J. Auster, and D.C. Schneider. 1995. A spatial and temporal perspective on research and management of groundfish in the northwest Atlantic. Reviews in Fisheries Science 3:201-229.

Lindholm, J.B., P.J. Auster, M. Ruth, and L. Kaufman. 2001. Juvenile fish responses to variations in seafloor habitats: modeling the effects of fishing and implications for the design of marine protected areas. Conservation Biology 15:424-437.

McCall, P.L. and M. Tevesz, editors. 1982. Animal-Sediment Relations. Plenum Press, New York.

Morrisey, D.J., L. Howitt, A.J. Underwood, and J.S. Stark. 1992. Spatial variation in soft-sediment benthos. Marine Ecology Progress Series 81:197-204.

National Research Council. 2001. Marine Protected Areas: Tools for Sustaining Ocean Ecosystems. National Academy Press, Washington, DC.

Nichols, A.O. and C.R. Margules. 1993. An updated reserve selection algorithm. Biological Conservation 64:165-169.

Peterson, C.H., H.C. Summerson, E. Thomson, H.S. Lenihan, J. Grabowski, L. Manning, F. Micheli, and G. Johnson. 2000. Synthesis of linkages between benthic and fish communities as a key to protecting essential fish habitat. Bulletin of Marine Science 66:759-774.

Polacheck, T. 1990. Year around closed areas as a management tool. Natural Resource Modeling 4:327-354.

Possingham, H.P., I.R. Ball, and S. Andelman. 2000. Mathematical methods for identifying representative reserve networks. Pages 291-305 in Ferson, S. and M. Bergamen, editors. Quantitative Methods for Conservation Biology. Springer-Verlag, New York.

Pressey, R.L, C.J. Humphries, C.R. Margules, R.I. Van-Wright, and P.H. Williams. 1993. Beyond opportunism: Key principals for systematic reserve selection. Trends in Ecology and Evolution 8:124-128.

Sherman, K., N.A. Jaworski, and T.J. Smayda. 1996. The Northeast Shelf Ecosystem: Assessment, Sustainability, and Management. Blackwell Science, Inc. Cambridge, MA.

Sherman, K., L.M. Alexander, B.D. Gold. 1993. Large Marine Ecosystems: Stress, Mitigation and Sustainability. American Association for the Advancement of Science Press, Washington, D. C.

Skinder, C.F. 2002. Marine protected areas in the Gulf of Maine: Policy for a common resource. M.S. Thesis. University of Maine.

Thackway, R. 1996. Developing Australia's Representative System of Marine Protected Areas: Criteria and Guidelines for Identification and Selection. Ocean Rescue 2000 Workshop Series, no. 2. Department of Environment, Sport and Territories, Canberra, Australia.

Valentine, P.C., T.J. Middleton, and S.J. Fuller. 2001. Sun-illuminated topography, and backscatter intensity of the Stellwagen Bank National Marine Sanctuary region off Boston, Massachusetts. United States Geological Survey Open-File Report 00-410, scale 1:60,000, 1 CD-ROM.

Zajac, R.N., R.S. Lewis, L.J. Poppe, D.C. Twichell, J. Vozarik, and M.L. DiGiacomo-Cohen. 2000. Relationships among sea-floor structure and benthic communities in Long Island Sound at regional and benthoscape scales. Journal of Coastal Research 16: 627-640.

ONMS CONSERVATION SERIES PUBLICATIONS

To date, the following reports have been published in the Marine Sanctuaries Conservation Series. All publications are available on the Office of National Marine Sanctuaries website (http://www.sanctuaries.noaa.gov/).

Benthic Habitat Mapping in the Olympic Coast National Marine Sanctuary (ONMS-06-01)

Channel Islands Deep Water Monitoring Plan Development Workshop Report (ONMS-05-05)

Movement of yellowtail snapper (*Ocyurus chrysurus* Block 1790) and black grouper (*Mycteroperca bonaci* Poey 1860) in the northern Florida Keys National Marine Sanctuary as determined by acoustic telemetry (MSD-05-4)

The Impacts of Coastal Protection Structures in California's Monterey Bay National Marine Sanctuary (MSD-05-3)

An annotated bibliography of diet studies of fish of the southeast United States and Gray's Reef National Marine Sanctuary (MSD-05-2)

Noise Levels and Sources in the Stellwagen Bank National Marine Sanctuary and the St. Lawrence River Estuary (MSD-05-1)

Biogeographic Analysis of the Tortugas Ecological Reserve (MSD-04-1)

A Review of the Ecological Effectiveness of Subtidal Marine Reserves in Central California (MSD-04-2, MSD-04-3)

Pre-Construction Coral Survey of the M/V Wellwood Grounding Site (MSD-03-1)

Olympic Coast National Marine Sanctuary: Proceedings of the 1998 Research Workshop, Seattle, Washington (MSD-01-04)

Workshop on Marine Mammal Research & Monitoring in the National Marine Sanctuaries (MSD-01-03)

A Review of Marine Zones in the Monterey Bay National Marine Sanctuary (MSD-01-2)

Distribution and Sighting Frequency of Reef Fishes in the Florida Keys National Marine Sanctuary (MSD-01-1)

Flower Garden Banks National Marine Sanctuary: A Rapid Assessment of Coral, Fish, and Algae Using the AGRRA Protocol (MSD-00-3)

The Economic Contribution of Whalewatching to Regional Economies: Perspectives From Two National Marine Sanctuaries (MSD-00-2)

Olympic Coast National Marine Sanctuary Area to be Avoided Education and Monitoring Program (MSD-00-1)

Multi-species and Multi-interest Management: an Ecosystem Approach to Market Squid (*Loligo opalescens*) Harvest in California (MSD-99-1)

www.ingramcontent.com/pod-product-compliance
Lightning Source LLC
Chambersburg PA
CBHW080354290526
45791CB00009BA/2873